ANGELA ROBERTS JONES

AFRICAN AMERICAN HISTORY MONTH

Daily Devotions

2014

Abingdon Press / Nashville

African American History Month Daily Devotions, 2014

Copyright © 2013 by Abingdon Press

All rights reserved.
No part of this work may be reproduced or transmitted in any form or by any means, electronic or mechanical, including photocopying and recording, or by any information storage or retrieval system, except as may be expressly permitted by the 1976 Copyright Act or in writing from the publisher. Requests for permission should be addressed to Abingdon Press, P.O. Box 801, 201 Eighth Avenue South, Nashville, TN 37202-0801, or emailed to permissions@umpublishing.org.

This book is printed on acid-free paper.

Library of Congress Cataloging-in-Publication Data

ISBN 978-1-4267-7374-7

13 14 15 16 17 18 19 20 21 22—10 9 8 7 6 5 4 3 2 1
MANUFACTURED IN THE UNITED STATES OF AMERICA

Introduction

One of the most awesome experiences in my life took place when I was a student at Fisk University. As a freshman, I was chosen to sing and travel with the Jubilee Singers. We continued the legacy of the original singers, who were former slaves and who traveled the world performing spirituals they had learned while in slavery.

The defining moment for me occurred just before my first concert. Standing in front of the portrait of the original Jubilee Singers in Jubilee Hall, we reflected on the history and then began to sing. All of a sudden, in the middle of the song, we were overwhelmed by the presence of God and the spirit of those singers who, by faith, had come out of slavery with determination to move forward. Before we could finish the song we began to weep. I found myself sobbing as I began to realize the trials of our people and how God had brought them out. The history, prayers, songs, struggles, and faith of my ancestors had leaped from the pages of history books and the mouths of storytellers into the depths of my heart. Words will never express that inspiration.

It is my privilege to write this devotional and focus on the legacy of faith, vision, perseverance, and purpose handed down to us from our foreparents. Black History Month is not only a time to reflect on the history of a people, it is also a time to fortify our faith. For if our ancestors could endure and achieve in spite of their circumstances, then surely we can have the kind of faith that will move mountains. Just as I, an African American, am inspired by stories of people of all cultures and backgrounds, I hope that every reader will be inspired by the biblical principles expressed on these pages, for these principles have no cultural boundaries.

I am thankful for my family, friends, and church families who have prayed for me and my children. But most of all, I thank God for the faith of my parents, the Reverend Beaufort and Mrs. Geraldine Roberts, who taught me how to pray and hold on to my faith. They taught my siblings and me not only to be proud of our heritage and fulfill our destiny but also to reflect the love of Christ beyond the walls of the church to all people.

—*Angela Roberts Jones*

The Faith Factor

Read Hebrews 11:1-7.

> *Faith is the reality of what we hope for, the proof of what we don't see.*
> **(Hebrews 11:1)**

Although you may not have the resources to fulfill your deepest desire, don't lose hope. There is a faith factor. To have faith means to believe and trust in God, who is sovereign, supreme, and Lord over all creation. The earth was created by God. It was spoken into existence by God. The substance by which the world was created came from God. If there is such a thing as evolution or a big bang theory, it is because God created the atom, the matter, the substance from which all things exist. If there was a bang, God was behind it.

Hebrews 11 chronicles the list of saints who believed this very thing. Therefore they obeyed God and trusted that what God spoke would happen. They couldn't see it, explain it, or reason it out, but they were assured of God's ability to work in them and for them.

Black History Month helps us understand that our ancestors embraced this very principle of faith. Many of them were brought to America with nothing. But God took nothing and made them (and us) into who we are today—musicians, craftsmen, entrepreneurs, politicians, educators, CEOs, generals, and so forth.

Just as we read of the patriarchs in Hebrews 11, by faith Benjamin Banneker became a self-taught mathematician, astronomer, and author; Dr. Charles Richard Drew pioneered blood plasma preservation; Granville Woods invented the telegraphony, a combination telephone and telegraph, and other electrical equipment that improved the nation's expanding railroad system; Ida Wells-Barnett became the most famous black female journalist of her time; Madam C. J. Walker became the first self-made millionaire businesswoman and the richest African American woman of her time. If they could do it—achieve, excel, and thrive in spite of circumstances—so can we.

God will provide what we need to fulfill our destiny. God watches over God's word so that God will perform it at the appointed time.

Prayer: *Lord God, I believe that you are willing and able to bless my life and make provisions. I will walk by faith and not by sight. Amen.*

The Power of Vision

Read Hebrews 11:8-19.

These all died in faith, not having received the promises, but having seen them afar off, and were persuaded of them, and embraced them, and confessed that they were strangers and pilgrims on the earth.
(Hebrews 11:13 KJV)

In 1846, a slave named Dred Scott had the audacity to sue in the St. Louis Circuit Court for his freedom. His argument was that he had resided with his master in states where slavery was illegal. So, in his mind, he figured that he should also be free. However, the decision of the courts—argued all the way to the U.S. Supreme Court in 1857—was that because blacks were not legal U.S. citizens, they could not sue in federal court. Therefore Dred Scott would remain a slave. On the contrary, this powerful vision of free blacks gave him the courage to challenge the system long before the Civil War, President Abraham Lincoln, and the Emancipation Proclamation. He embraced the possibility of freedom because, although the courts defined him as a slave, that is not the definition he embraced about himself.

Hebrews 11:13 explains that the people of faith listed in this chapter lived their lives based on a vision from God, even if that vision had not yet come to pass. Vision is the act or power of seeing, and the supernatural insight that comes from divine inspiration. God promised Abraham that Abraham would become the father of many nations and that his seed would be blessed. God also promised to give him Canaan, the land of promise. At the time of this promise, Abraham lived in the land of Ur, and his wife was barren. But, based on God's revelation, Abraham embraced God's plan and envisioned himself as God said.

What is your vision for your life? What have you embraced and what have you confessed or spoken over your life? Many of us have lost vision because we have embraced inferiority, mediocrity, poverty, loneliness, fear, anger, bitterness, hopelessness, and so forth. Don't fall in the trap of envisioning and embracing what others say about you. The world does not define you or your life, God does.

Prayer: *Lord, help me see beyond the limits I have placed on myself, and help me embrace your vision for my life. Amen.*

Yes, You Can!

Read Hebrews 11:20-30; 12:1-3.

So then let's also run the race that is laid out in front of us, since we have such a great cloud of witnesses surrounding us. Let's throw off any extra baggage, get rid of the sin that trips us up. **(Hebrews 12:1)**

The Scripture writer calls to mind the "cloud of witnesses" mentioned in Hebrews 11, people such as Noah, Abraham, Sarah, Moses, Jacob, Rahab, and others. All of them struggled through personal challenges, failures, or hardships on the way to fulfilling their destiny. Nevertheless, they continued to run the race of life with patient endurance.

We have modern-day witnesses. African American track and field athlete Wilma Rudolph was considered the fastest woman on earth in the 1960s. At the 1960 Rome Olympics, she became the first American woman to win three gold medals in a single Olympic Games event. In addition to being an African American in the segregated South, she had been paralyzed by polio at the age of four. She wore a leg brace until the age of nine, and an orthopedic shoe until she was twelve. Who would have thought that she would ever run, let alone become a track star?

Let me call two other witnesses to the forefront. Vashti McKenzie, the first female to be elected bishop in the African Methodist Episcopal Church, wrote a book some years prior titled *Not Without a Struggle*. Being a female in the ministry presents a separate set of challenges than those facing our male counterparts. Nevertheless, she endured, and is still moving strong. Also, Barack Obama was the first African American citizen not only elected president of the United States but also reelected for a second term. His slogan for his first campaign was "Yes, We Can." We must acknowledge the fact that, despite all odds, he persevered and won the election.

Facing challenges is not the issue, because, truthfully, we all do that. It is how we face those challenges that will determine our outcomes in life. There are two choices: success or unfulfilled purpose. It is comforting to know that Jesus, the author and perfector of our faith, has gone on ahead of us so that we can stand up and say, "Yes, I can—and I did!"

Prayer: *Lord, give me the stamina to endure the challenges I face in life. Amen.*

Fear Not and Do It Anyhow

Read 2 Timothy 1:6-9.

For God has not given us a spirit of fear, but of power and of love and of a sound mind. **(2 Timothy 1:7 NKJV)**

One of the most famous African American figures in history is Harriet Tubman. She is known as the "Black Moses" because she dared to make trips back into slave states to help lead slaves to freedom even after her own escape. Despite the risk of being captured, tortured, or murdered, she fearlessly led three hundred slaves to freedom through the Underground Railroad—without losing one life. Story has it that she threatened to shoot anyone who became fearful to the point of talking about going back to slavery. Harriet Tubman must have had a calling on her life. She did not allow fear to paralyze her dreams. She was determined to accomplish her mission.

In this Scripture, Paul admonishes Timothy to not give in to fear during a time of great persecution. Christians were being tortured and murdered in Rome for their faith. Paul encouraged Timothy to hold on to his faith and fulfill his calling as a pastor and evangelist. He told him not to be intimidated by the threat of persecution, even if it meant suffering through it.

Fear is a God-given emotion. There is natural or healthy fear of danger, and godly or reverential fear that is healthy. However, there is also an unholy or paralyzing fear, which is unhealthy. Do you have any fears? Are you afraid of getting a new job? Going back to school? Getting married? Remaining single? Forgiving your betrayer? Making a commitment? Giving yourself to the Lord—your past, present, and future?

Through the sacrifice of Christ, God has given power and ability to use your gifts and walk in your calling. God has given you love, not self-condemnation, the spirit of inferiority, or low self-worth. God has given you a sound mind—that is, the ability to make decisions from the mind of faith and the wisdom of God, even if you can't see the outcome. Fear is not the lack of apprehension to do something, but the courage to walk by faith in spite of your feelings of fear.

Prayer: *Lord, deliver me from my fears and give me the courage to step out on faith. In the name of Jesus, I pray. Amen.*

In the Meantime

Read Jeremiah 29; 33:3-8.

I know the plans I have in mind for you, declares the LORD; they are plans for peace, not disaster, to give you a future filled with hope. (Jeremiah 29:11)

The prophet Jeremiah admonished the children of Israel that they would be deported to the foreign land of Babylon. This would happen after the city of Jerusalem would be destroyed and the temple of God desecrated. Jeremiah prophesied that their set time of exile would be seventy years. However, in the meantime, the children of Israel were instructed to build homes, plant crops, and marry. God promised to not only protect them from further destruction from the enemy but to also bring full restoration at the appointed time.

We are aware of the fact that Barack Obama is the first African American president in the history of the United States, first elected in 2008 and reelected in 2012. But long before that, there were other bids for the White House by African Americans. The candidates include Lenora B. Fulani in 1988 and in 1992; the Reverend Jesse Jackson in 1984 and 1988; Congresswoman Shirley Chisholm in 1972; the Reverend Channing E. Phillips in 1968; and George Edwin Taylor in 1904. In addition, Blanche Kelso Bruce (born a slave in 1841) was nominated for the vice presidency in 1880, as was Frederick Douglass (born a slave in 1818) in 1872.

In other words, in between the time of slavery until the present—or in the "meantime"—African Americans did not wait on freedom in order to make positive and productive contributions. Even in the midst of oppression, they were helping build and shape America into the country it is today.

Beloved, there is a set time for your trials and tribulations. God is in complete control of when it begins and when it ends. But God's goal for you in the meantime is not to destroy you. At the appointed time, restoration and healing will follow this trial. The time in between your trial and your triumph is not "free-time" or "me-time"; it is God's time to work in you just as God did in the above examples. So be careful of how you spend your "meantime" by making sure that you give God his time.

Prayer: *Lord, give me the strength, courage, and wisdom to make it to my appointed time of deliverance. Amen.*

The Power of Grace

Read 1 Corinthians 15:1-11.

I am what I am by God's grace, and God's grace hasn't been for nothing. In fact, I have worked harder than all the others—that is, it wasn't me but the grace of God that is with me. (**1 Corinthians 15:10**)

One of the most best-loved and best-known hymns in the African American church is "Amazing Grace." I believe this song is so moving because, as a race of people, we understand our limitations and all of the things throughout history that worked against our progressing. For many African Americans, the conditions in early America were debilitating and humiliating. But still, African Americans achieved. However, we cannot credit these accomplishments solely to human beings. It was God's amazing grace that brought us out and enabled us to achieve what we have.

In this Scripture Paul recognized that, based on his past, there was no way he could have accomplished what he did in life. He was mentor to other pastors and apostles, he performed miracles, and he authored thirteen of the twenty-seven books in the New Testament. He was commissioned as an apostle to preach to the Gentiles. So you might say that Paul's ministry helped establish the New Testament church. But before that, however, he was a persecutor and murderer of Christians.

Similarly, many African Americans who paved the way for others had the challenge of tearing down walls to fulfill their purposes in life. Not focusing on their race as being a hindrance to moving forward were African American pioneers such as Marian Anderson, opera singer; Charles Reason, the first black college professor at a predominantly white American college; Bishop Richard Allen, founder of the African Methodist Episcopal Church; and Thomas L. Jennings, who patented the dry-cleaning process. Some of these pioneers did not receive any real formal training. But it is evident that their creativity and skill came from God alone. God gave them the ideas and the knowledge.

So no matter who you were yesterday or how you lived, you can be what God purposed you to be. God's grace will erase your past, and God's grace can work through your creativity, intelligence, and skill.

Prayer: *God in heaven, help me trust in your grace and not focus on my limitations. Amen.*

Take a Stand and Watch God Move

Read Ephesians 6:10-20.

Therefore, pick up the full armor of God so that you can stand your ground on the evil day and after you have done everything possible to still stand.
(**Ephesians 6:13**)

Have you ever been in a position in which you knew you were right, but the situation did not seem to work in your favor? Or have you experienced being totally misunderstood? Or had your good works spoken of as evil? Lately, I have spent a lot of time praying for and encouraging people who are facing adversity, especially in the workplace. Havoc is being caused by the supervisor, or co-workers are gossiping to the point that being in the same building is unbearable. Then there are those who are overlooked for a promotion despite their qualifications. Likewise, there are other situations where we know that we have every right to feel and act the way we do, but there is no validation in sight.

Rosa Parks, who is considered the mother of the civil rights movement, refused to relinquish her bus seat to a white passenger. According to state law, she was wrong; therefore the police were called and she was arrested. But according to God's law, she was right. She stood with the belt of truth that she was God's child, that all people are created equal in the eyes of God, and that, as God's children, we deserve to have certain rights and privileges. As a result of her determination to take a stand on that day, the Montgomery Bus Boycott followed, and the civil rights movement catapulted into a national event. After years of struggle, justice overpowered.

To stand simply means to be set or fixed on a certain attitude or position and not waiver from it. In the Scripture reading, Paul urges the readers to put on the full armor of God. The armor of truth, justice, peace, salvation, the word of God, and prayer will give you the strength you need to take a stand. There are some situations that we can do absolutely nothing about. It takes the power of God to actually turn things around. But if you put on the full armor and take a stand, God will fight on your behalf. Watch God move.

Prayer: *Lord God Almighty, I praise you for equipping me to stand. It is quite challenging at this moment, but I know that the battle is not mine but yours. Amen.*

How to Find Balance in Life

Read Ecclesiastes 3:1-22.

I know that there's nothing better for them but to enjoy themselves and do what's good while they live. Moreover, this is the gift of God: that all people should eat, drink, and enjoy the results of their hard work.
(Ecclesiastes 3:12-13)

Although I am now a full-time pastor, my first love is music. I started playing the piano at age six and spent most of my time either playing the piano and singing, listening to music, or reading. One of my favorite performers as a teenager was the popular rhythm and blues group Earth, Wind & Fire. As a young musician, I appreciated their harmonies and musicianship. Listening to their music was fun.

Later on, I enjoyed traveling and singing with the Fisk Jubilee Singers. The original singers during the 1800s were said to have introduced the African American spirituals to the world. These songs expressed the sorrow yet the spiritual depths of the African slaves. They were the slaves' avenue of expressing and bringing balance to the soul during and after slavery. As a matter of fact, the songs were so powerful that during the Jubilee Singers' tour in England, the queen stated the singers must be from the "Music City" of the United States. To this day Nashville is referred to as Music City.

What do you enjoy? Do you have balance in your life, or do you work and worry 24/7? An alarming number of people suffer from fatigue, stress, anxiety, and burnout. Even those of us who pray, read our Bibles, and attend church regularly tend to cave in to stress and anxiety.

The wise preacher addressed this issue in Ecclesiastes 3. There is a season for all things, good and bad. God has given us the special gift to enjoy the fruits of our labor. If we work hard, why not enjoy the life that God gave us? Sadly, many of us just don't know how to do that.

God has given us some positive avenues to bring balance and enjoyment to life. You have only one life to live, so I encourage you to intentionally search out ways to enjoy it. It just might save your marriage, your sanity, your friendships, and your life.

Prayer: *Lord, there are times of great demands and there are times to relax and enjoy the life you have given me. Give me the wisdom to flow in those seasons. Amen.*

Just Be Still

Read Psalm 46.

Be still, and know that I am God. (Psalm 46:10a NKJV)

> *Steal away, steal away, steal away to Jesus!*
> *Steal away, steal away home,*
> *I ain't got long to stay here.*

Have you ever felt that you were going in circles? Are you suffering from stress and anxiety? Do you even stop and take time to relax and appreciate your loved ones? Are you plagued with trying to make a certain situation work in your favor, but the more you try the more misunderstood you become? Well, maybe it's time to be still.

"Steal Away" is one of my favorite spirituals, especially the arrangement by Dr. Matthew Kennedy, my piano instructor and director of the Jubilee Singers at Fisk. Like many spirituals, this one also had a dual meaning. The coded meaning in this song was a call for the slaves to secretly meet to plan their escape or to share information. The spiritual meaning reflected the slaves' deep longing and expectation to live eternally with Jesus. Many had come to the resolve that even if they personally never came out of slavery, their only fight was to stay in relationship with Jesus Christ their Savior.

Now let's relate this to Psalm 46. To be still means to actually stop striving and to hear and trust God. Many times we spend so much time and energy trying to reverse things and nothing changes. In verse 1, God as a refuge is likened to a place of hiding or shelter from the natural elements. The psalm also addresses national and worldly concerns that may be out of our control.

You may not need a physical shelter, but you need a spiritual one. You can commit your soul, thoughts, emotions, and concerns to God through prayer and faith. You can let it all out and trust God's intervention. You can steal away in your mind and change the direction by replacing negative thoughts with thoughts of God's love and power! There is a place of peace and assurance that comes from God alone. Be still.

Prayer: *Lord, help me recognize situations I cannot do anything about. Give me wisdom to make decisions and do what I can. The rest I leave in your hands. Amen.*

Dare to Be Different

Read Galatians 2:15-21.

I have been crucified with Christ and I no longer live, but Christ lives in me. And the life that I now live in my body, I live by faith, indeed, by the faithfulness of God's Son, who loved me and gave himself for me.
(**Galatians 2:20**)

The Negro spiritual "Lord, I Want to Be a Christian" shows that our forebears were not preoccupied with their oppression but had a real relationship with Jesus Christ. The verses reflect this: "Lord, I want to be more loving in my heart" and "Lord, I want to be like Jesus in my heart." I personally made a decision a long time ago to live a life of holiness and purity, not because I am called to be a minister but because my first calling is to be a Christian. We are called out from the world, and we must dare to be different.

But in this day and time this is not the popular thing to do. To be "crucified with Christ" means that we may lose friends who are uncomfortable with our choice. It also means to put to death those lusts and desires that oppose biblical principles and to make the living Christ the center of your life.

In this passage, Paul's identity as a keeper of the law was in opposition to his being a receiver of the gospel of Jesus Christ. Paul had been a murderer and persecutor of Christians, believing that they were to conform to his belief about God and way of living. But Paul was transformed by the gospel of Christ. Therefore he crucified, or put to death, the old Paul and allowed his lifestyle to reflect his choice to live according to the teachings of Christ.

Some of us mistakenly believe that if we make this commitment, we will not be able to enjoy life, relationships, or prosperity. We are afraid that we will miss out on life because of the boundaries that we feel come from committing ourselves to Christ. A godly lifestyle is not a matter of perfection, but decision. And I am here to tell you that although it is a process to get there, it is well worth it to come to a point where Jesus Christ is truly the head of your life. I dare you to be different.

Prayer: *God of all mercies, strengthen my heart and order my steps as I seek to live a life that is pleasing to you. Amen.*

Your Purpose-Driven Life

Read Psalm 139.

You are the one who created my innermost parts; you knit me together while I was still in my mother's womb. I give thanks to you that I was marvelously set apart. Your works are wonderful—I know that very well. My bones weren't hidden from you when I was being put together in a secret place, when I was being woven together in the deep parts of the earth. Your eyes saw my embryo, and on your scroll every day was written that was being formed for me, before any one of them had yet happened. **(Psalm 139:13-16)**

One of the 2012 Kennedy Center honorees was African American blues guitarist Buddy Guy. The son of a sharecropper, he grew up picking cotton. At an early age, he made a guitar from the wire of a window screen. *Good Morning America* tells the story that one of his ex-wives told him that he would have to choose her or the guitar. Of course he chose the guitar. One might ask why he would make that choice. The answer is simple: the guitar was linked to his purpose. I am not encouraging divorce. But we must understand that a person cannot successfully be separated from his or her purpose. Life and purpose are a package deal.

In this psalm, David understood that God knew him from the inside out because God is Creator. After many overwhelming trials, David surrendered his soul to God to search him out from the innermost and lead him to the path that was already laid out by his Maker.

Are you wrestling with why you are even here on this earth? Many people make self-destructive decisions because they just can't see the purpose of life. But if you have breath, you have purpose. Before you were formed as an embryo in your mother's womb, God purposed that you would first live and then God purposed everything about you. God formed you from nothing into a living being. If you are struggling with life and with what to do next, read and meditate on this psalm. Your life is unique, and your purpose is custom-made by God.

Prayer: *Lord, thank you for my life and for purpose. I know that you created me and fashioned my days. Examine me, look at my heart, and lead me through this journey. Amen.*

Prayer Does Change Things

Read Psalm 143.

Listen to my prayer, LORD! Because of your faithfulness, hear my requests for mercy! Because of your righteousness, answer me!...My spirit is weak inside me—inside, my mind is numb. I remember the days long past; I meditate on all your deeds; I contemplate your handiwork. **(Psalm 143:1, 4-5)**

When I was a child, my parents made sure that our family ate breakfast together every Sunday morning. We each had to quote a Scripture before joining hands in prayer. There were other times that we prayed together but, without fail, family prayer was required before we went to church on Sunday. This prepared me as an adult to lean and depend on God by praying through all of my life's decisions, trials, and triumphs. In my painful moments prayer has sustained me. Thank God for praying parents.

In this psalm, David prays for guidance and deliverance from his persecutors. Overwhelmed by the stress of betrayal and persecution, he knew that God could and would do something about it. He put his trust in God Almighty.

Negro spirituals such as "Every Time I Feel the Spirit" and "I Couldn't Hear Nobody Pray" express one of the key elements to the perseverance of black folk in struggles: prayer. Our foreparents talked to the Lord about everything. They prayed for strength and courage. They prayed for freedom. They prayed for their children and for their relationships. They prayed for their enemies and oppressors. They prayed for their country and the president.

Through prayer they connected with God as God's children. Through prayer they were empowered through the Holy Ghost. Through prayer they experienced a peace and joy that could not be destroyed by injustices. Through prayer many created and excelled in every area of life imaginable. Through prayer their faith was strengthened, they had visions of a bright future, they understood God's purpose for life and for mankind, and they understood the power of Jesus' dying on the cross for their sins.

The same principles of prayer apply to you. I challenge you to try it and trust God.

Prayer: *Lord, thank you for the privilege of prayer. You made a way for our foreparents, and you will do it for me. Amen.*

No Longer Bound

Read Galatians 4.

In the same way, when we were minors, we were also enslaved by this world's system. But when the fulfillment of the time came, God sent his Son, born through a woman, and born under the Law. **(Galatians 4:3-4)**

On January 1, 1863, President Abraham Lincoln issued the Emancipation Proclamation declaring that all slaves in the Confederate and rebellion states during the Civil War would be forever free. The institution of slavery, which began in the American colonies in the 1600s, was coming to an end. However, the process for real freedom in American society has extended years beyond the Civil War and the signing of a document.

This reminds me of my neighbor's dog, which is probably close to ten years old now. Much of his life has been spent either in the house or, when outside, chained to a fence. Recently I have noticed that although he is no longer chained to the fence, he does not leave the yard. Even when my neighbor is not at home, the dog still stays bound to the yard.

Likewise, a person in bondage cannot exercise his or her own will but is totally subject to the will of something or someone else. We are all mentally enslaved to something—whether good or bad. What dominates your thinking or your decision making? What are you passionate about? What do you desire most? A few bondages that can cripple the mind, body, and soul are bad relationships; negative thinking; an uncontrollable tongue; anger; pain and depression; fear; drug, alcohol, and even food addictions; and low self-esteem. Some are big and some are small. But bondage is bondage.

Jesus died on the cross to set us free. He has already purchased our freedom with his own blood. Our faith in him has given us the status of a son or daughter. The Holy Spirit confirms this. As a child of God, we do have the power to overcome any hindering bondage. The starting point is your faith that Jesus has already made it possible. If you have not already begun the process of freedom, start today—but stay the course. You will succeed because your Emancipation Proclamation has been signed in red—*Jesus.*

Prayer: *Dear Lord, thank you for making a way for me to be free of my bondages. I set my eyes on the goal of freedom as I walk through this process. Amen.*

Now Help Free Someone Else

Read John 4.

Many Samaritans in that city believed in Jesus because of the woman's word when she testified, "He told me everything I've ever done." So when the Samaritans came to Jesus, they asked him to stay with them, and he stayed there two days. Many more believed because of his word, and they said to the woman, "We no longer believe because of what you said, for we have heard for ourselves and know that this one is truly the savior of the world."
(John 4:39-42)

Do you realize that your life could be a blessing to someone else? In September 1862, President Abraham Lincoln issued a warning to the Southern states in rebellion against the Union that the Emancipation Proclamation would go into effect on January 1, 1863. It was at this point that President Lincoln issued specific authority to the U.S. Army to recruit and train colored soldiers. By the end of the Civil War, nearly two hundred thousand colored soldiers—known as the United States Colored Troops—had fought to retain their own freedom as well as to obtain freedom for other African slaves. The liberated had become liberators.

No matter who we are, we have all been delivered from something. The woman at the well in John 4 had an encounter with Jesus. He helped her come to a resolve with her past and sinful relationships, and he explained who he was and what he was sent to do. The woman believed Jesus and received him as the Messiah. She then went to the village to share her testimony. "Come, see a man," she said (v. 29 KJV). And guess what? They came and were set free by the gospel of Jesus Christ. Her testimony is all she had to bring others to freedom in Christ.

Three months after my husband passed away, I was affirmed as church pastor. The same comfort I received from God is what I imparted to others. What about you? What are you waiting on? It doesn't take institutional credentials to share your testimony, especially if you are moved by the Spirit of God. Your testimony may be exactly what someone else needs to move forward.

Prayer: *Lord, thank you for keeping my soul through the pain and past failures of life. Today, I purpose in my heart to use the good and the bad of life to encourage someone else. Amen.*

Looking Back, but Moving Forward

Read Philippians 3:1-14.

I myself don't think I've reached it, but I do this one thing: I forget about the things behind me and reach out for the things ahead of me. The goal I pursue is the prize of God's upward call in Christ Jesus. (Philippians 3:13-14)

One of the first things we learn to do as new drivers is to use our rearview mirrors. The rearview mirror reminds us where we just traveled and assures us that we are indeed moving forward. It also helps us stay alert to other traffic so that we can avoid being hindered in any way from arriving at our destination safely. But the key to safe driving is to glance back yet stay focused on moving forward.

Black History Month is a time to reflect on past struggles and celebrate victories and accomplishments. A lot has happened, but we can't park here. A prolific example is that of Booker T. Washington and his book *Up from Slavery*. The overall message was to help African Americans achieve higher education and financial goals by becoming knowledgeable about the U.S. educational and economic systems. He focused on race relations to help his race and the state of America at that time in its transition from slavery to equality. He met with President Theodore Roosevelt and became the first African American to dine with a U.S. president.

In his letter to the Philippians, Paul reflects on his life. From the beginning of the chapter, he lists admirable accomplishments. But he realizes that there is a better way, another opportunity to move forward, an open door to improve his life as one who was called by God. In order to move forward, he says that he must forget the past. In essence, to forget simply means to adopt a new life and a new attitude. He was determined to lay ahold of the new life presented to him through the gospel of Jesus Christ.

Beloved, when you know to do better, then you must do better. Drop pride and stubbornness and let go of those things that have no relevance to moving forward. Then you must reach for what has been revealed as moving forward. Don't park here! God has more for your life.

Prayer: *Lord, empower me to look back without regret, but move forward with purpose. Amen.*

Make an Adjustment

Read Isaiah 43.

> *Don't remember the prior things; don't ponder ancient history. Look! I'm doing a new thing; now it sprouts up; don't you recognize it? I'm making a way in the desert, paths in the wilderness.* **(Isaiah 43:18-19)**

Are you ready for something new? Are you ready for a change? I have heard the song "Precious Lord, Take My Hand" sung at many funerals and church events in my lifetime. It was written by Thomas Dorsey, who is known as the father of gospel music. Dorsey combined the styles of blues and jazz music with the gospel and Baptist hymns, resulting in a sanctifying beat with drums and other instruments. The style was new at the time and rejected by many churches. But it was eventually embraced, and has become a blessing to the body of Christ.

Isaiah prophesied a new thing that God was about to do in the lives of the Israelites. The first half of the book of Isaiah speaks about judgment and punishment for the Israelites' rebellion against God. In this verse, Isaiah prophesies full restoration, reconciliation, and deliverance to the Israelites. In ancient times, God had delivered them from Egypt and led them through the wilderness. In spite of their rebelliousness, they did not go without food or water. But now God would restore in a new way. The prophet was preparing their hearts for deliverance through the person of Jesus Christ. This restoration was a new thing.

Losing my spouse after nearly twenty-five years of marriage was a major adjustment. I knew the very day he died that life for me would not be the same. Every single area of my life—emotionally, physically, and spiritually—was affected by the traumatic blow. But as I sought the Lord for healing, the Holy Spirit revealed to me that the sooner I made adjustments in all of the necessary areas at the necessary times, the easier my journey to healing and wholeness would be. With the help of God, I began to slowly embrace new possibilities and a new life.

Beloved, you won't always be in the state that you are in. As God moves you from trials to triumphs, or perhaps from poverty to prosperity, adjustments must be made. God is doing a new thing—and it might just be better. Adjust.

Prayer: *Lord, thank you for this new thing you are doing in my life. Amen.*

Live, Laugh, Love

Read Psalm 16 and Proverbs 15:13; 17:22.

You teach me the way of life. In your presence is total celebration. Beautiful things are always in your right hand. **(Psalm 16:11)**

At the dawn of the twentieth century, W. E. B. DuBois wrote *The Souls of Black Folk.* In his book he describes the sorrow of the past; the struggles to move out from the darkness of slavery; the quest to become educated as a race; the task to train African American political leaders who would represent black people in the "other world"; and the sorrow songs known as Negro spirituals, which expressed the weariness of heart but also a faith in God that freedom was inevitable.

DuBois described the "twoness" of the African American: the soul that was free, gifted, intelligent, creative, and loved life, but was tormented by the chains of the outward circumstances of bondage. Inside of this human being lies dormant a desire to enjoy a fulfilled life. In essence, it doesn't matter about your race, culture, education, or economic status, the human soul has a need to live, laugh, and love.

I sought to fulfill this need even in the middle of my own sorrowful experience. I believe that many faithful Christians and non-Christians alike have forgotten to fulfill this basic human need. Solomon, who was considered the wisest man on earth, emphasizes in Proverbs 17:22 that the road to healing is a joyful heart. To have joy means to take pleasure or delight in something. To find that pleasure or happiness, one must search out the good and learn to be content. Furthermore, the author of Psalm 16 acknowledges God as the one who will teach what life really is all about. To learn this, one must be in God's presence. In God's presence we learn to celebrate life. This brings a heart of joy and laughter.

So a sure cure for sorrow and depression is to laugh and to learn to celebrate life. Maybe you need to take another approach to life. Go to the movies or take a vacation. Go somewhere you have never been, or do something you have never done. Make some new friends. Love those in front of you while you have them. It's good medicine for the soul.

Prayer: *Lord, I have one life to live. It's time for me to celebrate the gift of life. Amen.*

Consider the Big Picture

Read 1 Corinthians 12.

So the eye can't say to the hand, "I don't need you," or in turn, the head can't say to the feet, "I don't need you."... If one part suffers, all the parts suffer with it; if one part gets the glory, all the parts celebrate with it. You are the body of Christ and parts of each other. (**1 Corinthians 12:21, 26-27**)

If you have ever put a puzzle together, you know that the picture is not complete until you have every single piece in the correct place. Each piece neatly locks with another piece whose grooves correspond with those of the piece next to it. It is difficult to put a puzzle together without first studying the big picture. Once you get that picture etched in your mind, the memory will help you work through the puzzle pieces.

This same principle applies to every single person on earth. We each have a gift and something to offer. Paul sought to encourage the Corinthian church by admonishing them of the fact that no one gift in the body of Christ was more important than another. The fact that some of the gifts seemed more prolific, or their functions more visible, did not mean that the less noticeable gifts were not important.

Likewise, in regard to history, African American history is *American* history. Hispanic American history is *American* history, and so it is with every other race of people who have migrated to or been birthed within these shores. We have all contributed to America's existence in some form or another. Carter G. Woodson, the father of black history and the first to formally study African American history, did not insist on the designation of February in observance of African Americans in order to cause further segregation, but rather to show the world how this race of people fit into the big picture to lead to further advancement.

Within every individual lies the desire to understand how one's life fits into the big scheme of things. Our true purpose is just like a puzzle piece that locks into the puzzle piece of someone else's life. If you are searching for the meaning and value of your life today, then take the time to check out the puzzle pieces around you. You may be surprised at what you will discover about yourself.

Prayer: *Lord, I know that my life has purpose and meaning, regardless of my age, race, or economic condition. As I transition through life, reveal your plan to me. Thank you for my life. Amen.*

Prayer for Peace in Relationships

Read Ephesians 4:1-16.

Accept each other with love, and make an effort to preserve the unity of the Spirit with the peace that ties you together. You are one body and one spirit, just as God also called you in one hope. (**Ephesians 4:2b-4**)

Today's devotion is a prayer for peace in all relationships, such as with spouses, families, church families, friendships, and coworkers. There seems to be so much conflict and offense in the world. If you are struggling in a relationship, today is the day for a breakthrough.

An important fact that we should not forget as we observe Black History Month is that black Americans were not the only ones fighting for their freedom. There were numerous non-blacks who joined forces to fight against an unjust system. One such group was the Freedom Riders during the 1960s. They challenged the laws of segregation by putting interracial pairs and black riders on buses or other modes of public transportation that were segregated. They gained national attention and helped bring Jim Crow laws to an end. But the beauty of it all is this: the common thread of unity that caused this mix of races to risk being jailed and killed was their common belief that equality was God's plan for America. This was a community united by beliefs.

Ephesians 4 speaks of unity being maintained by focusing on the common belief of one body, one Spirit, one God, one hope, one Lord, one faith, and one baptism. Paul admonishes the Ephesian church to diligently and deliberately focus on this unifying theme. The purpose of the church leadership was to make sure the body of Christ understood why they were who they were, and God's plan to bring the body of Christ to maturity and unity of faith.

Now what is the main thing, the glue that holds relationships together? Whether in churches or in marriages, it is our beliefs, love, purpose, and respect. Are you taking the time to focus on the common thread that first brought you and the other person (or people) together? Peace and harmony don't just happen; they take work and a conscious choice to remain united, no matter what.

Prayer: *Dear Lord, saturate my mind and my thoughts with your purpose for this relationship. Bring us to the unity of the common faith in you as we conduct ourselves in a manner that is pleasing to you and respectful to others. Amen.*

Forgive and Let It Go

Read Matthew 18:21-35.

"Lord, how many times should I forgive my brother or sister who sins against me? Should I forgive as many as seven times?" Jesus said, "Not just seven times, but rather as many as seventy-seven times." (**Matthew 18:21b-22**)

Jesus instructs his disciples to always forgive. In this parable, after the servant had begged forgiveness from his master of a debt the servant could not pay, the servant would not forgive those who were indebted to him. Instead of receiving retribution from the offenders, he received rebuke from the master and was turned over to the torturers. This is a warning from Jesus that the same thing will happen to those who will not forgive.

The strength of the civil rights movement led by Martin Luther King, Jr. was nonviolence. He preached that one could not dispel hate with hate, but that love and forgiveness were the keys to overcoming injustice. In retrospect, we must admit that if African Americans—or anyone else faced with disfranchisement—did not act on this very principle of forgiveness, this country would have self-destructed from hate and violence. The future prosperity of this nation is hinged on forgiveness.

This principle is true for every individual struggling with forgiveness. Unforgiveness will not only ruin present and future relationships but it will also cause internal torment in the one who will not forgive. Before we can move on and clear our minds of the offense, we have to let it go. Remember these principles:

1. Forgiving does not mean that you deny what happened.

2. Denying the offense will not make it go away.

3. Dealing with the offense openly and in love opens the door to true healing. It helps the offended one release the offender.

4. Forgiving is not simply forgetting, and forgetting is not simply forgiving. To forget means to acknowledge the wrong and release the offense to God, trusting God to handle it. In time the offense will no longer control or consume your thoughts. Giving it over to God in prayer will release your emotions and bring peace to your soul.

Prayer: *Lord, empower me to forgive and release this offense. Bless my offender with your presence, so that both of us can move on. Amen.*

Don't Let the Devil Steal Your Joy

Read Nehemiah 8:1-12.

"Go, eat rich food, and drink something sweet," he said to them, "and send portions of this to any who have nothing ready! This day is holy to our LORD. Don't be sad, because the joy from the LORD is your strength!"
(Nehemiah 8:10)

In this narrative told in Nehemiah, the people had returned to Jerusalem after seventy years of exile in Babylon. They had rebuilt the wall of Jerusalem. As they gathered to hear the word of God as read by Nehemiah, they were convicted by their actions and God's mercy, and began to weep. They were reminded of their painful ordeal and recognized that God had watched them, even in their ignorance and rebellion of God's requirements. Nehemiah's response was to encourage them to go and celebrate and be joyful. At this point, that would bring them the strength to move forward, not the sorrow of reflecting on their bad decisions and their rebellion against God. In other words, don't cry over spilled milk; it's just time to fill up another bucket.

Beloved, don't let the devil steal your joy. You may have messed up, struggled, sinned, wasted time, or whatever, but stop right now and count your blessings, praise God that things are as good as they are, and focus on your future. You see, the devil wants you to believe that you have so many faults and weaknesses that you will never be able to succeed, that you have screwed up so many times that God's forgiveness has run out, that you have hurt so many people and they will never forgive you, and that you might as well give up because there is no way to fix this mess. But today is the day to rebuke these thoughts and focus on God's almighty power to heal, save, set free, and deliver you from any and all situations.

Yes, God does deal with sin and evil, but God also forgives. God is merciful, faithful, kind, loving, and true. God extends grace and mercy to those who may not even deserve it. Nehemiah's command to the people was to respond to the word of God, to go forth from this point in time and put it into action. That command remains relevant today. God's joy will restore your joy.

Prayer: *Lord, I thank you for a second chance. Infuse me with your joy and your strength so I can continue this journey. Amen.*

Face Your Giants

Read Numbers 13 and 14.

> *"The land that we crossed over to explore is a land that devours its residents. All the people we saw in it are huge men.... We saw ourselves as grasshoppers, and that's how we appeared to them."*
>
> ...
>
> *"If the LORD is pleased with us, he'll bring us into this land and give it to us.... So don't be afraid of them."* (**Numbers 13:32b-33b; 14:8a-9b**)

Four days after Martin Luther King, Jr. died, his widow, Coretta Scott King, led a peaceful march with her four children through the city of Memphis, Tennessee. Not only did she go to the physical place where a murderer had been able to kill her husband but she also had to painfully visit a place where the father of her children was taken away from her. This took incredible courage. She did not let the mountainous giants of fear and pain discourage her from continuing on with the vision spoken through her husband and the civil rights movement. This was God's plan, and she would continue to march on to freedom.

Well, we have in this Scripture the story of the Israelites who were commanded by God to enter the promised land of Canaan, a land flowing with milk and honey. But the bad report given by ten of the twelve spies was that there were giants in the land whom the ten spies were certain they could not overtake. The giants caused the spies to focus more on their limitations than on God's promise to be with them. But two of the spies encouraged the others to possess the land; however, the Israelites would have to fight for it. They would have to face the giants one way or another. Fear dominated faith, and the Israelites ended up wandering in the wilderness for forty years.

Today you may be facing a giant. Maybe you need to confront the issues that are causing your marriage to fall apart. Or maybe it is some other uncomfortable situation. Or maybe it's a bad habit. Whatever it is, if you don't face your giants, every day spent in the wilderness is a day taken away from what has been promised to you. Remember God's promise of peace and prosperity in your promised land.

Prayer: *Lord, today I choose to focus on faith and not give in to my fears. My giants do not cancel out your promises. I declare this in your name. Amen.*

Peace: The Cure for Worry

Read Philippians 4:6-9.

***Don't be anxious about anything; rather, bring up all of your requests to God in your prayers and petitions, along with giving thanks. Then the peace of God that exceeds all understanding will keep your hearts and minds safe in Christ Jesus.* (Philippians 4:6-7)**

Years ago, jazz singer Bobby McFerrin recorded "Don't Worry, Be Happy," which quickly hit the charts and became the first *a cappella* song to reach number one on the *Billboard* charts. The song simply addresses all types of adverse situations that happen in life, but consistently repeats the message "Don't worry, be happy."

To worry means to be tormented or to suffer with persistently disturbing thoughts. Many people today suffer from depression and insomnia because they are tormented with concerns. The opposite of worry is peace. To be at peace means to be in a state of harmony, to have freedom from anxiety and obsessive or irritating thoughts, and to be in a state of calmness or serenity.

In this scripture, the cure for worry and anxiety is to first pray and share all of your concerns with God. It really helps to talk to someone and get the thoughts out of your head. But sometimes the only one to share with is the Lord. Whether you have friends or not, share all of your requests and even your deepest desires with the Lord through prayer. It is also all right to plead and to ask over and over again. This doesn't mean that you are questioning the sovereignty of God, but it means that you are taking the matter to the one who will listen and can do something about it. Praying is therapeutic.

As you pray and share your requests, thank God for God's faithfulness and intervention. God may not change your situation, but God can and will give you peace that does not come from human reasoning or understanding. This peace will surface even if your situation doesn't change. Philippians 4:8-9 lists positive things to focus your thoughts on: all that is true, holy, just, pure, lovely, and worthy of praise. In other words, with the help of God you can redirect your thoughts. This is the whole prescription for peace. Take it daily for it to take effect.

Prayer: *Lord, thank you for the cure for worry and anxiety. Amen.*

A Changed Mind

Read Ephesians 4:17-32.

> *But you didn't learn that sort of thing from Christict.... Instead, renew the thinking in your mind by the Spirit and clothe yourself with the new person created according to God's image in justice and true holiness.*
> **(Ephesians 4:20, 23-24)**

In 1972, the United Negro College Fund adopted the marketing slogan "A Mind Is a Terrible Thing to Waste." This phrase became a household saying. It was effective in inspiring African Americans to get an education to change their mind-set from the oppression of the past to open doors of prosperity and progression in the future. According to statistics, the number of college-educated African Americans increased.

The phrase hit the nail on the head; all decisions and vision for life begin in the mind. You really can't move beyond your mind-set. I compare the mind to the operating system of a computer. There is the hardware, the operating system, the application software, and the user. The user can only make the computer do what it is programmed to do. The operating system determines the functionality of the computer.

How do you operate? What's your mind-set? We have a certain way in which we operate. We have been programmed by our parents, the world, and all of life. But Scripture addresses our inner self in regard to our spiritual convictions. It helps us take inventory of not just our confession, but our conduct. One of the biggest struggles I have witnessed as I minister to people is how to change their behavior so that they can practically walk out their faith. The way to make a change is to make a decision that you are not satisfied, and then investigate what your behavior should be. Further in the passage, today's Scripture reading addresses honesty, anger, bitterness, our speech, kindness, compassion, and forgiveness. Our relationship with others is just as important as our relationship with God.

Don't let your past turn your present into a waste. Be strong and make a change.

Prayer: *Lord, I thank you for a renewed mind and another chance to make a change. I may not be what I should be, but I thank you that I am not what I used to be. Amen.*

A New Start

Read Psalm 51.

Create a clean heart for me, God; put a new, faithful spirit deep inside me! Please don't throw me out of your presence; please don't take your holy spirit away from me. Return the joy of your salvation to me and sustain me with a willing spirit. Then I will teach wrongdoers your ways, and sinners will come back to you. **(Psalm 51:10-13)**

Everybody makes mistakes. We all have made bad decisions and offended someone at some point in our lives. We must take responsibility for our lives and for the mistakes we make. Why? Because there are consequences. Everything we go through is not someone else's fault. Is this not what we teach children?

It is not the end of the world. There is an opportunity to start new and fresh. God does forgive and empowers us to start over. The Negro spirituals "Fix Me, Jesus" and "Standing in the Need of Prayer" express the need to turn the searchlight inward and allow God to heal the heart. To sin means to miss the mark. But God has provided a way to turn your life around and to live God's way. It's simply called repentance.

That's what David did in this psalm; he repented. He had committed adultery with Bathsheba, and there was a baby on the way. But David, known as a man after God's own heart, humbled himself before God. He realized that in order to become successful in his calling and purpose as king and prophet, he had to turn his heart back to God and seek cleansing of his actions, mind, and soul. David admitted his fault and earnestly sought forgiveness. He realized that the issue was not between him and the world, but between him and God. He needed the Spirit of God to accomplish his life's goals, so he sought God.

You may not be able to relate to David's sin, but perhaps there is an issue in your life that you know needs to be dealt with. God is ready to renew, refresh, and restore your life, but is just waiting on you. It's time for a fresh start.

Prayer: *Lord, it's me at this moment standing in the need of prayer. I take responsibility right now for any and all of my wrongs. Forgive, cleanse, and heal me. In the name of Jesus I offer my life. Amen.*

Stay in the Fight

Read 2 Timothy 2:1-13.

> *So, my child, draw your strength from the grace that is in Christ Jesus.... Accept your share of suffering like a good soldier of Christ Jesus. Nobody who serves in the military gets tied up with civilian matters, so that they can please the one who recruited them.* (**2 Timothy 2:1, 3-4**)

Although I have never been in the military, I have had the opportunity to observe soldiers through my job as a teacher in the schools at Fort Campbell, Kentucky. I have also ministered to and observed active-duty and retired soldiers, along with their families, in our church as well as in my own family. I have seen soldiers and their families deal with the effects of war. The tragedy of 9/11 and the Iraq and Afghanistan conflicts have really made me appreciate our military. I believe we should celebrate and pray for our military every chance we get.

The traditional song "I'm a Soldier in the Army of the Lord" helped African Americans understand what it means to endure hardships. The verses say "I got my war clothes on in the army of the Lord" and "If I die, let me die in the army of the Lord." In essence, our foreparents understood that the fight was not a physical one, but a spiritual one of two kingdoms—that of God and that of the devil. Their quest was to remain faithful to God the Creator.

In this Scripture, Paul admonishes Timothy to draw strength from Jesus Christ in order to endure the hardships. Like soldiers at boot camp, Timothy was training for war. In the military, boot camp trains the person to think like a soldier. The recruit must learn to use a weapon and go without the luxuries of home and a civilian life. He or she must learn to operate as a unit and stay focused on the mission. Soldiers learn to receive and obey orders from their superior officers of the same army.

In the army of the Lord, we are to understand that the conflict is the "fight of faith" (1 Timothy 6:12), and it is internal. The battle is in the mind and heart, *Should I trust God in this struggle or not?* The weapons of our warfare are spiritual: prayer, fasting, worship, praise, the word of God, and faith. As soldiers we must learn how to use our weapons and stay in the fight. After all, the battle is already won.

Prayer: *God Almighty, I will not give up, but I will pick up my spiritual weapons and fight. Amen.*

We Survived!

Read Romans 8:28-39.

Yet in all these things we are more than conquerors through Him who loved us. (Romans 8:37 NKJV)

A few years ago I had a chance to visit the African American history museum in Detroit. One of the displays was a replica of a ship that transported slaves from Africa to America. Such ships would cross the Atlantic Ocean on the route known as the Middle Passage. The ship would contain the bodies of African men and women in heinous conditions, lying below deck on shelves arranged like kitchen cabinets. They would be packed like sardines. Some Africans survived the Middle Passage, while others did not. I left the museum utterly speechless and choked up by what I saw.

Looking at America today, we can see that the seed of these men and women not only survived, but is still thriving. Those slaves helped make America the great country it is.

Perhaps you have survived your own "middle passage"—that is, any painful experience that it took God above to bring you through. You may have suffered through a bad divorce, rape, molestation, domestic abuse, or a drug or alcohol addiction. Maybe you have been the victim of a crime or witnessed someone you loved gunned down or murdered. I myself suffered through witnessing my spouse have a fatal heart attack.

But somehow, some way, we made it. Romans 8:35-39 lists hardships in life that many people may suffer. Because we are conquerors through Jesus Christ who loved us, God will work everything out for our good. Whatever did not kill us made us stronger. Whatever did not take our minds gave us more wisdom. Whatever did not consume our emotions gave us more love and compassion.

If you haven't already done so, take that challenging "middle passage" of your life and use it as a stepping-stone to a bigger and brighter tomorrow.

Prayer: *Lord, thank you for allowing me to survive my middle passage. It wasn't the beginning of my life, and it is surely not the end. Amen.*

In Celebration of Our "Roots"

Read Matthew 1.

A record of the ancestors of Jesus Christ, son of David, son of Abraham:...So there were fourteen generations from Abraham to David, fourteen generations from David to the exile to Babylon, and fourteen generations from the exile to Babylon to the Christ. (**Matthew 1:1, 17**)

In Genesis 1:1 and John 1:1, we see the beginning of all things and the divine roots of Jesus, the Son of God. But the root of Jesus Christ as the Son of Man began as Matthew recorded Jesus' genealogical line. Jesus' ancestry can be traced through forty-two generations. Not all listed were men, not all were of Jewish heritage, and not all were squeaky clean. Some of the family members were jacked up and dysfunctional, but God used ordinary people to fulfill God's purpose in laying a foundation for a family that would nurture God's only begotten Son.

In 1977, the powerful eight-part television miniseries *Roots* premiered. It was based on the book *Roots*, by Alex Haley. The miniseries chronicled the history of Haley's family from Africa through slavery in America and freedom. This dramatization transformed television and enlightened America on the experiences of slavery.

The church I now pastor was founded in 1865 by former slaves who secretly held their worship services in a brush arbor. The congregation was established as the First Colored Baptist Church in New Providence, Tennessee, and later became known as Greenhill Missionary Baptist Church. My home church, in Sylvania, Georgia, has similar beginnings. Founded in 1865 by former slaves as Simpson Chapel, it later branched off to become St. Andrews United Methodist Church. These are powerful roots. Roots are important.

Like a hardy tree, we too have roots that run deep and keep us grounded. Thank God for our biological and spiritual families. Without them where would we be? Most of all, thank God for our faith that is rooted in Jesus Christ, through whom we are more than conquerors. I pray that through these devotions you have been inspired to continue being grounded and rooted in your faith.

Prayer: *Lord, thank you for the privilege and the opportunity to celebrate our heritage. Help us to never forget our roots. In the mighty name of Jesus Christ. Amen.*